IMAGES OF ENGLAND

# BIRMINGHAM PUBS

IMAGES OF ENGLAND

# BIRMINGHAM PUBS

KEITH TURNER

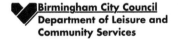

First published 1999
Reprinted with revisions 2002, 2004, 2008, 2013

The History Press
The Mill, Brimscombe Port,
Stroud, Gloucestershire, GL5 2QG
www.thehistorypress.co.uk

British Library Cataloguing in Publication Data.
A catalogue record for this book is available from the British Library.

ISBN 978 0 7524 1809 4

Typesetting and origination by
Tempus Publishing Limited.
Printed and bound England.

# Contents

# Acknowledgements

I should like to thank, once again, my former colleagues in Birmingham Central Library for showing such forebearance in the face of the disruption occasioned during the compilation of this book. Special thanks must also go to all those local photographers whose prints are gathered in the library; without their earlier endeavours this compilation would never have been possible.

# Introduction

This book is personal.

Ever since I came to work in Birmingham some forty years ago I have been entranced by the sheer number and diversity of its pubs. Some were grand and opulent, some were rough and unwelcoming but most were ranged somewhere in between those two extremes. There and then I resolved to visit as many of them as possible – a self-appointed labour of love not yet completed – for, with the best will in the world, a plan to visit a certain number on a free day would often be sabotaged by finding the first one so enticing that any thoughts of moving on would be quietly forgotten. There was, after all, always another day. But there wasn't: many of the pubs I intended to visit have been closed – even demolished – as the city was subjected to yet another phase of regeneration and 'modernisation'. Some changes were of course inevitable – but some were sheer civic or commercial vandalism.

One hundred years ago there were more than 1,500 hotels, inns, taverns and public houses in Birmingham. These terms are all familiar ones – but what exactly do they denote? Traditionally, hotels offered accommodation to strangers but did not necessarily serve alcoholic beverages while taverns and inns offered alcohol and overnight lodgings; public houses were simply houses whose owners had a licence to sell alcohol to passers-by. Licences were issued by local magistrates and subject to periodic renewal. The term 'bar' was used to denote a licensed room in a hotel or a building of another nature entirely, for example a theatre. Together, all such establishments went by the general description of 'hostelries'. Today these terms are used fairly indiscriminately with 'tavern', 'bar' and 'inn' being popular revivals for made-over pubs. Examples of all of these are portrayed here.

A licence could be for the sale of all types of alcoholic drink, or just for beer – in late-nineteenth century Birmingham, over two-thirds of all licences were of the latter kind, no doubt indicative of the working class' preferred tipple. In the 1870s over ninety-five per cent of its pubs brewed their own beer. Outside Birmingham, the picture was much the same. A century later, home-brew pubs had all but disappeared with only a handful remaining in the whole of England, eagerly sought out by real ale enthusiasts. (Today, home-brew pubs are on the rise again, a movement aided by the availability of off-the-shelf micro-breweries, though they will never represent more than a tiny fraction of the total beer market.) How did this reversal come about? The answer lies in the sudden realisation by a number of pub-brewers that, by expanding their operations greatly, they could supply other pubs as well as their own. So, in the 1880s, companies were formed and capital invested with the result that by the mid-1890s the number of home-brew pubs in Birmingham had shrunk to well under twenty-five per cent of the total. The rest obtained their beer from one or other of the local 'common brewers' of which, in 1890, there were forty in Birmingham and neighbouring Smethwick.

Another radical change accompanied the death of the home-brew pub: the idea of the tied house. What better way could a brewer have of securing guaranteed outlets for his beer than by owning the pubs that sold it? By 1890, in Birmingham, the Holt Brewery had 155 licensed houses, Henry Mitchell had 86, and Ansell & Sons 64. The other two large Birmingham breweries at the end of the century were Davenports, registered in 1896 with 57 pubs and Atkinsons who, two years later, had more than 80. That year saw the merger between Henry Mitchell, a Smethwick brewer who had opened Cape Hill Crown Brewery just beyond the Birmingham boundary in 1879, and William Butler, another Smethwick brewer who had begun brewing in partnership with his brother-in-law at the Crown on Broad Street (see p. 9) in 1875.

From then on Mitchells & Butlers (M&B) and Ansells vied with each other as to who was the largest of the region's brewers as a period of expansion, takeovers and mergers saw the smaller independents swallowed up by the larger brewers who then turned their attentions upon each other. The Holt Brewery Co. (formed in 1887) became part of Ansells in 1934 (and the Holt squirrel became part of the new Ansells trademark), M&B acquired Atkinsons' Aston Park Brewery in 1959 and, in the following year, William Butlers of Wolverhampton (who had taken over Frederick Smith's Aston Model Brewery in 1955). Earlier M&B acquisitions were Cheshire's Windmill Brewery in Smethwick in 1914 and John Charles Holder's brewery in Nova Scotia Street, Birmingham, in 1919.

Inevitably, outside commercial and financial factors now came into play. Long gone were the days when a brewer could only supply beer to a region bounded by how far and back a horse-drawn dray could travel in a day. Motorised transport on improved roads meant great areas of the country could now be supplied and regional brewers vied with each other for potential markets. In 1961 the country's first national brewery combine appeared when Allied Breweries was formed by the merger of Ansells, Ind Coope and Tetleys, closing its Birmingham brewery twenty years later. Davenports' brewery, located on Bath Row and famous for its home delivery service, was taken over in 1986 by Greenall Whitley – and promptly shut, leaving Birmingham – the second largest city in Britain – in the remarkable position of possessing not a single brewery within its boundaries!

But what of the city's pubs? Their evolution and development closely mirrors that of the breweries. In the mid-nineteenth century they were, architecturally, very much in tune with their surrounding buildings, usually being adaptations of older houses or cottages in town or village. Then, in the 1890s, with the rise of the common brewers, a radically new type of pub appeared. Either a rebuild of a former hostelry, or a new construction entirely, they were easily identifiable by their lavish use of terracotta and ornamentation outside, and of sumptuous tiling, mirrors, wallpaper, stained glass and other embellishments inside. Partly a reflection of the new-found wealth of the brewers and partly a response to the puritan streak in local government at the time seeking to regulate the drinking habits of Birmingham's inhabitants, these 'reform' pubs can still be found liberally scattered around the city. A growing number of them are now listed buildings as their importance is, at long last, properly appreciated.

Next came the rise of the roadhouse – a catch-all term which, for the sake of this book, has been applied to pubs sited on main roads that relied heavily on passing trade for their custom. With the rise of private motoring between the wars, and the creation of large housing estates in the suburbs, their numbers exploded in a brewery-driven bid to tap new markets; again, they were either new buildings entirely or enlargements of old ones. The years after the Second World War saw the construction of a number of new pubs, often on new housing estates and of a singularly unattractive, featureless design involving much dull brick and concrete walls, flat roofs and large, unadorned windows. Sadly, their construction was often at the expense of older, far more attractive buildings elsewhere as part of the trade-off for obtaining a new licence was the promise on the part of a brewery to close down a couple of existing pubs. That said, it is perhaps best to draw a veil over this dismal episode in the history of Birmingham pubs and be prepared to welcome, with an open mind, its latest phase. As mentioned at the end of Section Six, a new period of pub-opening recently took place in the city centre. How it turns out is anybody's guess; perhaps, in a hundred years' time, people will look back on photographs of the pubs of the 1990s with the same mixed emotions as they look at those of the 1890s today. One thing is certain – the history of Birmingham's pubs is still being written, just as it ever was.

# One

# Taverns in the Town

*Even though their details may be unrecorded, it is safe to assume that ever since Birmingham has existed there have been taverns to serve its inhabitants. Indeed, they would have served an ever-increasing number of non-residents as people journeyed into market from the surrounding countryside, or changed horses or stagecoaches here (and later trains), or called on business regarding any one of the thousand trades for which Birmingham was renowned. In the centre of the town (it did not become a city until 1889) customers would snatch a bite to eat, or sink a pint or two after – or even during – work, discuss the day's news, conduct a spot of business – legal or not so legal – or wait for the theatre to open. Much the same as today in fact.*

The Crown Inn, on the corner of King Edward's Place, as it was in 1781. The lane it faced onto later became Broad Street, the main thoroughfare leading westwards out of the city centre. The licensee was John Owen. As a youth, William Butler worked here as a part-time barman. The pub still stands, though rebuilt and later much modified, trading as the Reflex '80s Bar' Bar & Diner.

The Old Crown, Deritend High Street, 1850s. The licensee from 1853 to 1858 was Thomas Dayson, whose name appears over the doorway on the far right; he was succeeded as publican by his widow Ann. The corner of the premises nearest the camera is occupied by James Wheeler's butchers shop. This is a familiar image but is included here simply because of the building's claim to be the oldest in Birmingham. Supposedly dating from 1368, it is unlikely that any of the original structure remains today, though what there is is certainly very ancient in parts. During the 1980s and 1990s its future was very uncertain – being some distance from the city centre put it at a distinct disadvantage – and it was even closed for a while, but a thorough refurbishment has given it a new lease of life. After several years' neglect in the 1990s, it is once again open for business following a thorough refurbishment.

The Dog & Duck in Holloway Head, 1868. The brick tower, the remains of Chapman's windmill which stood behind it, appears as a ghostly shadow on the original photograph.

The Greyhound Inn cider house, on the corner of Holloway Head and Marshall Street, 1964. The notice announces that the landlord, M.V. Beard, is 'Licensed to Brew'. Popular in the 1960s for its cheap but potent ciders, it escaped demolition unlike most others in the area (see Section Six) but has undergone a succession of reconstructions encompassing the whole corner block (to the left of photo), its latest incarnation being no longer a pub, but a strip club.

The Old Leather Bottle in Deritend High Street, *c.* 1885. Immediately beyond it is the Three Crowns; both premises were probably conversions of two private houses. Leather bottles were a common means of storing liquids before the Industrial Revolution made the production of cheap glass containers possible. Together with leather pitchers, also much used in early alehouses, they were commonly known as 'leather jacks'. The pub name Three Crowns is generally thought to allude to the Three Kings or Magi of the Nativity story or, just possibly, to King James I and VI of England, Scotland and Wales.

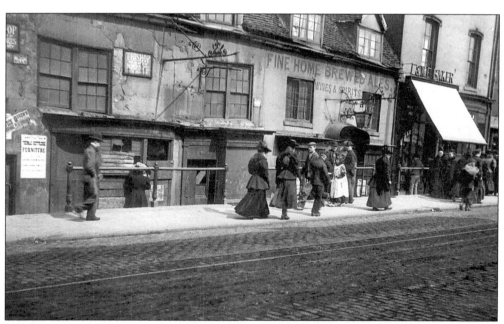

The Old Leather Bottle as it was in 1900. It was demolished in 1901 having closed ten years earlier.

The Ship Inn on the corner of Sandy Lane and Camp Hill. Established in 1560, it was commandeered by Prince Rupert, nephew of King Charles I, in 1643 during the Civil War as his Birmingham headquarters. The licensee at the time of the photograph was T. Turner. East India Pale Ales are advertised – these were brewed in Burton-upon-Trent of sufficient strength and purity to withstand the long sea voyage to India for the benefit of the troops and government officials out there.

The Ship Hotel, 19 June 1971. This rebuild of the Ship Inn was demolished shortly after the photograph was taken, hence its boarded-up condition. Note the statue of Prince Rupert above the doorway.

The Rodney Inn in Coleshill Street, Dale End, pre-1857. The proprietor was Henry Holder who also ran the Concert Hall next door. In 1857 the latter was extended and the frontage greatly altered. The Rodney was almost certainly named after Admiral Sir George Brydges Rodney (1719–92) who famously defeated the French fleet off Dominica in 1782 in the West Indies, it being a common practice to name – or rename – pubs in honour of military leaders, or great victories of the day.

Dudley Street, 1895. Here were located R.J. Bradshaw's dining rooms where Holder's beers were served and the BEST 6d DINNER IN BIRMINGHAM advertised. Such establishments blurred the distinction between restaurants and pubs; a century later the wheel had turned full circle with many city centre pubs relying on the sale of lunchtime food to keep them in business.

An advertisement for Holder's Brewery Ltd from an 1890s Prince of Wales Theatre programme. The firm's Midland Brewery was in Nova Scotia Street, near Curzon Street, not very far from the city centre.

# HOLDER'S ALES

ARE BREWED WITH THE

## Choicest Malt & Hops

AND PURE

## ARTESIAN WELL WATER.

TERMS ON APPLICATION AT THE

## MIDLAND BREWERY,

## BIRMINGHAM.

The Golden Lion, Deritend High Street, probably towards the end of the nineteenth century when the pub was still in business. The right hand third of the building is occupied by Joseph Lees, a general cooper, whose sample wares can be seen in the window and hanging outside. The building is thought to date from around 1600.

The Golden Lion, c. 1908. The pub is now derelict but was saved for posterity when it was dismantled brick by brick and re-erected in Cannon Hill Park in 1911.

The Golden Lion in Cannon Hill Park, c. 1970. It is currently undergoing long-term restoration.

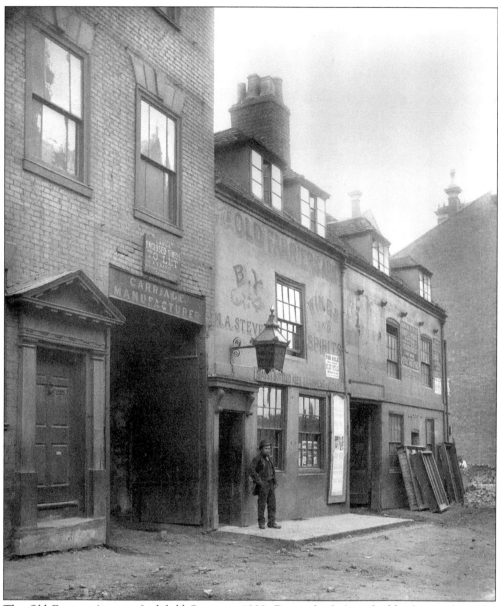

The Old Farriers Arms in Lichfield Street, *c.* 1880. Dating back (as a building) to at least the eighteenth century, it was opened as a pub in the 1840s by George Jones, a livery-stablekeeper – a farrier being a shoer of horses. Lichfield Street was razed to make way for the new Corporation Street, completed in 1903.

The Waterloo Bar on the corner of New Street and Christ Church Passage, *c.* 1890. The building immediately beyond is the Royal Birmingham Society of Artists' gallery (opened in 1829). The lettering on the upstairs windows publicises the fact that billiards can be played here – as if the large wooden sign was not enough! – and that public and private rooms were available; the ground floor windows proclaim it to be a free house, i.e. not tied to one particular brewery.

An 1878 advertisement for the Waterloo Bar, as printed in E. Edwards' *The Hen and Chickens Hotel, Birmingham,* a pamphlet history published that year.

# THE WATERLOO BAR,

## CHRIST CHURCH PASSAGE,

### BIRMINGHAM.

The Proprietor begs to announce the **completion** of his extensions, which have been carried out in a **style unequalled** in the Provinces, and not surpassed by **anything of its class** in London.

#### THE FITTINGS AND DECORATIONS

Are from designs by Thomas Verity, Esq., **London,** (Architect of the Criterion), and the Tile permanent decorated Walls and Ceiling have been executed by Messrs. Minton, Hollins and Co., Stoke-upon-Trent.

#### COLD LUNCHEONS, CHOPS, STEAKS, SOUPS, &c.
ARE NOW PURVEYED.

The Red Lion Hotel in Church Street, 1886. The licensee was one H. Nicholas, selling Alfred Homer's beer from the Vulcan Brewery in Tower Road, Aston. A fly-poster on the wall advertises a mass meeting – but for what? Rebuilt some twenty years later, its fine replacement has been named the Old Royal since the 1960s.

The Apple Tree in Dudley Street towards the end of the nineteenth century. In keeping with its name, it advertises cider as well as perry and beer.

The King's Arms that once stood on the corner of Suffolk Street and Hinckley Street, 1897. Home-brewed beer and Burton ales are advertised.

The same pub about ten years later, now proclaiming itself to be a Holder's establishment, much extended around the corner. Both Suffolk Street and the King's Arms are now long gone.

The Comet in the old Bull Ring, 1895. The pub is only one narrow room wide, not an uncommon feature in the days of piecemeal development and a sure supply of customers – as would be the case here. On the right is the statue commemmorating Nelson's victory at Trafalgar, erected in 1809, moved to a site by the Outdoor Market in 1961 but now back where it belongs following the redeveiopment of the Bull Ring in the 2000s.

Inside Birmingham's Weights and Measures Department in St Martin's Lane, 1901. Then, as now, the serving of short measures was an offence and marked vessels would be supplied to pubs to keep landlords in line. Here pewter pint pots are being stamped – 'struck' – with the verification of their capacity.

Earthenware jugs for the licensed trade were also marked, this time in the open air using a sandblasting machine. Such items are today avidly sought after by collectors of breweriana.

The Wheatsheaf Inn, Suffolk Street, 1895. The licensee was Alfred Darwent.

The Bull's Head on the corner of Smallbrook Street and the Horse Fair, probably in the 1900s. It provides a contrast in size with. . .

. . .the Greyhound Inn close by in Navigation Street, seen here about the same time.

The Star Wine Vaults, Dale End, 1898. Despite its name, stout on draught and Allsopp's 60-shilling bitter are being advertised. Hungry office and shop workers requiring a more substantial midday meal are catered for at the Royal Exchange Luncheon Bar next door.

The same establishment, just a few years later. Having dropped the 'Wine' from its name, the pub windows now advertise whisky! One of Birmingham's new electric trams is creeping out of shot on the left. The pub later expanded into the luncheon bar, with a new ground floor façade unifying the whole.

The Old Pump Tavern, c. 1890. Not all the town centre pubs were grand structures with frontages on a busy street; many could be found in the older parts of the town tucked away down alleys and in the corners of yards, as was the case with this drinking-hole in the Bull Ring.

An advertisement for the Hen & Chickens, as printed in an 1890s Prince of Wales Theatre programme. This was a famous Birmingham pub which (probably) began life in the early eighteenth century as a hotel and posthouse in the High Street – where it even had its own bowling green! (Bowling was closely associated with pubs and many Midland taverns boasted their own greens. A few still do – see Section Three.) At the very end of the century the business was transferred to more elegant premises in New Street close to the Grammar School.

The Leopard Inn on the east side of Great Hampton Street, Hockley, 1901. Squeezed in on the right is the workshop of D. Jones, die and press tool forger and general smith.

The Drovers' Arms by the Horse Market in Moat Row, 20 July 1901. The two steam tram trailers in the background on the right, behind the horses and donkey, indicate that a centuries-old way of life, reflected in the pub name, is changing rapidly. Just two days later this area was enclosed as an extension of the covered Vegetable Market. The building was a converted eighteenth-century house while the roadway was named after Peter de Bermingham's twelfth-century moated manor house.

Lower Temple Street, November 1901. Here was located the side entrance to the Pit Bar of New Street's Theatre Royal in the days when an evening at the theatre was very much a part of the working man's night out on the town.

The entrance to the Pit Bar in close-up. This and the next six photographs were all taken in November 1901.

The back of the Pit Bar as seen from Stephenson Street. In the foreground is the yard entrance to the theatre's Gallery Bar.

Inside the Pit Bar – about as basic a drinking den as can be imagined.

Slightly more up-market was the Gallery Bar – but only just. The landlord certainly lives up to his name in terms of self-promotion!

The grander Circle Bar for the richer, socially superior class of theatre-goers. Note the bottles of Bass on the counter with their distinctive red triangle on the labels – the very first registered trade mark.

If you thought the Pit Bar was basic, this was the wine cellar beneath the theatre...

...with patrons seated on empty crates!

# GEORGE TAYLOR,

## Hockley Brewery,

## BIRMINGHAM,

# ALE ALE

### AND

# PORTER

## BREWER,

### From the Choicest Malt and Hops, and Pure Artesian Well Water.

---

## ESTABLISHED 1833.

---

*Special Terms to the Trade.   Private Families Supplied.*

An advertisement for George Taylor's products, as printed in a Prince of Wales Theatre programme of the 1890s. His Hockley Brewery was located in Nursery Terrace, Hunters Lane.

The Bull's Head Hotel on the corner of Smallbrook Street and the Horse Fair after rebuilding, 1912. (Compare with the photograph on p. 24.) The staff living quarters are on the first floor, guests' bedrooms on the second and the kitchens on the third – presumably housed there because of lack of space on the ground floor. Cheshire's beers (from Smethwick) are advertised as being on sale.

The Hope & Anchor in Edmund Street, probably during the 1950s. Like several of the city centre pubs, it boasted a separate restaurant to cater for the lunchtime demands of the working population. The demand for food is still the same today, only now the vogue is for mixed eating and drinking in the same room. This end of Edmund Street was razed in the 1960s to make way for the Paradise Forum complex.

Stevens Bar on the corner of the High Street and New Street, 1951. What was a simple but attractive ground floor façade has been totally dominated by a massive electric advertising sign of remarkable vulgarity. Happily, the sign went when this whole block was rebuilt at the end of the decade but, sadly, so did the pub.

In complete contrast, the Beaconsfield Hotel, Aston, 1878. Before merging with Birmingham in 1911 Aston was a Municipal Borough in its own right and, as a consequence, had its own complement of town pubs, several of which could rival any that its larger neighbour had to offer. One such was the magnificent Beaconsfield Hotel, located on the High Street, New Town.

The Longboat, Brindley Wharf, *c.* 1975. One of the last of the city's purpose-built pubs, the Longboat was constructed during the 1960s as part of the redevelopment of the area immediately to the north-east of the civic centre. (One of the problems met with when trying to promote Birmingham as a player on the world stage is its lack of a photogenic river or seashore, hence the modern-day concentration on its canal system.) The derelict premises between the canal basin and Cambridge Street were remodelled as Brindley Walk and the new pub given a canal theme inside – and the wrong name! It should, properly, have been called the Narrowboat. Hugely popular during the 1960s and 1970s, especially at weekends and on live folk music nights, it went into a gradual decline during the next decade (along with the folk scene). Formerly the Flapper & Firkin, it is now simply the Flapper, noted for its live music nights..

Also on the High Street in Aston stands the Bartons Arms, seen here in the 1970s. Although often threatened with demolition it has, unlike the Beaconsfield Hotel, survived and is now perhaps Birmingham's most famous pub; for many years it has certainly been its most decorated. It was opened by M&B in 1901 and has been relatively untouched since (though some opening-out has been done.)

Restoration work underway on the outside of the Bartons Arms, 1980. The future of this grand old pub is, at least for the present, secure. For many years a theatrical pub, it quenched the thirsts of the staff, performers and patrons of the Aston Hippodrome behind it – including, or so legend has it, that of Charlie Chaplin when performing there with Fred Karno's company.

Where a lot of Birmingham's beer came from: inside the semi-automatic brewhouse at Ansells' No. 2 Brewery, Gosta Green. This was the old Holt's brewery, rebuilt in 1965 but closed just seven years later. (The offices became the Pot of Beer pub.) The large vessel in the left foreground is a wort holder where the water and malt was boiled with the hops.

And where a lot of it went: University of Birmingham students on one of their Carnival floats, 1936. Universities and beer have always gone together – indeed, they would have originally brewed their own. With three universities now in the city, the association is destined to continue for a good while yet.

# Two

# Backstreet Boozers

*The backstreet pub is, alas, of a dying breed. Once the Victorian inner city was full of them, flourishing on every other street corner – and often halfway down the streets in between as well. Usually small and unpretentious, they represented the original definition of a pub, being little more than an ordinary terraced house with a couple of rooms on the ground floor adapted for the sale and consumption of beer and spirits, and the playing of traditional pub games such as darts, cribbage and dominoes. Yet the backstreet boozer was more than just a place to relax – it was often the sole focal point of social life within a tiny working class community otherwise preoccupied with the unremitting round of toil and drudgery that was its lot. Then, as slums were cleared and roads widened, as grand office blocks were erected and small factories closed, so these pubs began to disappear one by one as the city centre expanded. The process continues to this day with those furthest from the centre tending to survive better – though not always as pubs. Take a stroll through any remaining area of Victorian terraced housing and the chances are that, on at least one street corner, the unmistakable architectural details of a present-day shop or house will give away the secret of its former life.*

Cambridge Street, 1928. An ordinary-looking back street, remarkable only for the fact that it was just a stone's throw from the city's civic centre. The Prince of Wales pub, middle distance, still stands – though now in the shadow of the International Convention Centre built directly behind it. The suspicion is that it escaped demolition because it was the lunchtime local for the Planning Department! Ironically, its traditional interior was gutted in the 1990s in an act of commercial vandalism.

Park Street, Digbeth, just two or three days after the Murphy Riots of 1867. Only the three-dimensional sign of the phoenix rising from the flames denotes that the large building next to W. Broughton's stables and cart manufactory is a pub. Curiously, despite appearing to be of relatively recent construction, the pub was even then officially called the Old Phoenix Inn. The licensee at the time was Ralph William Corner. The Murphy Riots were the violent reaction to a visit to Birmingham by William Murphy, a noted anti-Catholic preacher of the day.

Jamaica Row, *c.* 1890. Number 28 in this thoroughfare, off Edgbaston Street in Smithfield, was the Woodman – a popular name for Birmingham pubs, as shall be seen, with no less than seven hostelries of that name listed as being open in 1899.

The King's Head in Allison Street, Digbeth, on 14 May 1906. As proclaimed by the painted sign, this was once a home-brew pub though at the time of the photograph it was awaiting demolition as part of the area's slum clearances.

The Bell Hotel at No. 60 Lozells Road, c. 1900. Grander than the average backstreet pub, its size meant that it could boast a number of attractions not found in smaller establishments. To begin with, there was a billiards room where pool and pyramids could also be played (these last two games were the forerunners of snooker) while the two makeshift signs in the window to the left display the names of the forthcoming Smoking Concert attractions (left) and announce that the Lozells Debating Society met there every Sunday evening at 7.30pm (right), presumably in an upstairs Function Room. Possibly standing outside in the group of staff and customers is the licensee, George Albert Asbury.

The Anchor Inn on the corner of Rea Street and Bradford Street, probably in 1902. Posing in the doorway is the licensee George Edwin Benwell and his wife Emma. Formerly a brassfounder like his father, Benwell took on the Anchor in 1902 when he retired from that trade. The conveniently-sited tram stop right outside the front door was no doubt of great benefit to his customers in all weathers – and states of drink! The pub was rebuilt in the reform style shortly after and remains comparatively unchanged to this day.

The Stag & Pheasant in Gosta Green, c. 1930. Another corner pub, this was located at the junction of Woodcock Street and Heneage Street, the licensee in 1930 being Herbert Charles Thomas. Smaller than the pub in the previous photograph, it would have comprised a public bar plus a smoke room or snug on the right. Painting a pub's name on a side wall was a common practice, to announce its existence to anyone approaching from that direction; more unusual is the apparent lack of a sign on the front of the building, though the painted brewer's sign there does include a depiction of M & B's famous leaping stag trademark – perhaps this was thought to be enough, given the name of the pub?

The Cambridge Inn, 1928. Another Cambridge Street pub, this stood on the corner of Crescent Wharf. It appears to be boarded-up in readiness for yet another phase in the never-ending redevelopment of this street.

The Swan with Two Necks at the end of Aston Street, Gosta Green, on 10 February 1932. The name is a fairly common English pub name and is a corruption of the more rarely seen 'Swan with Two Nicks' – a reference to the swan-upping practice of marking swans' beaks to denote ownership. The splendid hanging lamps and brackets are worthy of note. The licensee in 1932 was Walter Henry Hawkins; two years later the present-day fire station occupied the site.

Emily Street, Highgate, *c.* 1934. Slum houses are being demolished to make way for St Martin's Flats while the Emily Arms, on the corner with Dymoke Street, awaits its turn.

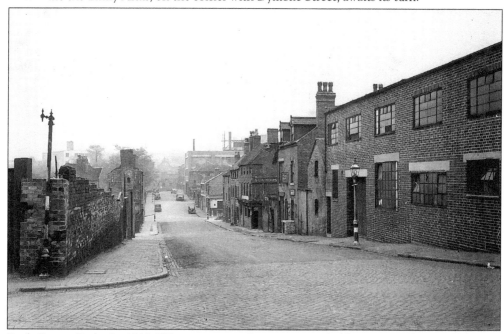

Buck Street, Digbeth, 1945. What appears to be an unremarkable corner pub named the Sea Horse is in fact a coffee tavern. These non-alcoholic alternatives to more traditional taverns were a legacy of the flourishing temperance movement of the late nineteenth century but, by the time of the Second World War, they had all but disappeared. A similar fate was about to befall the Sea Horse with the razing of the area. Ironically, this was a former home-brew pub, its beer once famously known as 'Digbeth Water'.

Almost in the city centre itself, this was the Green Man on the corner of Weaman Street and Sand Street, by Snow Hill, again in 1945 before the post-Second World War redevelopment of the area. The licensee is given as Mary Ellen Symes.

The Sacks of Potatoes, Gosta Green, summer 1950. A popular Birmingham pub to this day, especially with the students from the neighbouring universities of Aston and Birmingham City. After being put to a variety of uses – including a period as that quintessential 1960s institution, an Arts Lab – the former Delicia cinema next door is now a bookshop. The pub, once a multi-level, multi-roomed delight has not been so fortunate, having been ruined in recent years by the removal of its internal walls, partitions and screens.

Not too far away on the ground, but a considerable distance in style and clientele, was the Old Nelson, on the corner of Great Lister Street and Rupert Street (date of photograph unknown). A very basic pub – but an honest working class one. Saltley gasworks is in the background and was once a major source of customers for the pubs of the area. Both the pub and the gasometers have now gone, and the whole area redeveloped.

The Shakespeare Inn on St Marks Street, Spring Hill, 1964. It is seemingly closed for good, awaiting demolition as part of the redevelopment of the whole area now bisected by Ladywood Middleway.

The Dolphin in Irving Street, 1954. The words on the first floor windows indicate that the pub once boasted a Club Room. The licensee at the time of the photograph was Sylvester Patrick Byrne.

Again recorded for posterity before demolition in 1964, the Marquis of Lorne in Cecil Street in New Town is the first of a trio of late-Victorian period grand corner pubs all similar in overall appearance but very different in their architectural details.

The Bull's Head on the corner of Bishopgate Street and Tennant Street, just off Broad Street, again in 1964. The then licensee was Albert Frederick Hall. Designed by James and Lister Lea, and opened in 1901, it was closed (and gutted) during the late 1990s but reopened as the City Tavern, with its interior sympathetically refurbished.

The Woodman in Digbeth, on the corner of Albert Street and New Canal Street, 1975. Another typical Lea design, it was built by Ansells in 1897 with an interior of Minton tiles. It reopened in 2013 after several years of neglect and threatened demolition.

Less imposing, but more than making up for its lack of stature with its wonderful external tiling, this was the Craven Arms on the corner of Blucher Street and Gough Street in 1965. It looks virtually the same today with its heavy blue tiling, the building extended (at the rear) but not ruined. The neighbouring houses were about to be replaced by industrial units. It is now part of the growing Black Country Ales pub chain.

The Gough Arms on the corner of Gough Street and Marshall Street, 1964. Another survivor, it is located just a few yards from the Craven Arms – the two buildings can scarcely be more different in appearance, especially since its 2007 interior and exterior makeover.

The corner of Coventry Street and Allison Street in Digbeth, 15 November 1904. If there was not a pub on a backstreet corner, the chances were that the site would be occupied by a general store, often licensed to sell alcohol. Outwardly, this building could easily be mistaken for a backstreet pub – especially with its enormous Mitchells & Butlers advertisement – but that is not too surprising: when such terraces of houses were constructed, the developer would often build the corner unit to a larger design with a view to letting or selling it as either a shop or pub. With the decline of this type of public house after the Second World War, some were converted into shops of all kinds, and some into houses; many though were demolished as part of slum clearance programmes, as in this particular instance.

# Three

# Village Inns

*As anyone who has lived in the city for any length of time knows, Birmingham is made up of a city centre surrounded by a number of former villages which, over the years, have been brought within its expanding boundaries and generally incorporated into one great urban sprawl. Once, however, these villages were separate entities in their own right and, as with villages all over England, had as their twin focal points the church and the pub. Often both buildings would be in extremely close proximity, and both played their vital part in the celebration and commemoration of a never-ending circle of christenings, marriages and burials. At all other times, a pint or two and a chat with friends was just as much a part of the Sunday ritual as the church service beforehand and the roast dinner afterwards.*

The Dolphin Inn on the Warwick Road, Acocks Green, 1927. The licensee was Mrs Alice Pagett.

A closer view of the inn. The sign calls it the Old Dolphin Inn – evidence of antiquity, real or imaginary, has long been regarded as a good selling point in the pursuit of customers.

The (new) Dolphin Inn, 1934. This building has just replaced the old Dolphin with a new side road, Victoria Road, added as part of the redevelopment. The next side road past the pub is Dolphin Lane. The pub closed in 1992 and a supermarket now occupies the site.

The Coach & Horses Inn, Castle Bromwich, 1927. A 1*d* in the slot weighing machine is visible in the porch. The pub has since been rebuilt.

Ye Olde Green Man, Bromford Lane, Erdington. This is another pub with a (justified) name claim to antiquity. The weighing machine in the forecourt would appear to be for checking deliveries. The licensee in 1899 was George Birbeck.

The Roe Buck Inn at No. 132 Erdington High Street, *c.* 1906. The ornate lamppost outside also carries the overhead wires for the new electric tramway into Birmingham, opened the following April (with this narrow High Street section replaced by a stretch along the Sutton New Road in 1938). The licensee in 1906 was Albert Lees – very probably the gentleman in the doorway on the far left, with his wife in the doorway in the centre.

The Swan, also in Erdington High Street, 10 February 1952. It was replaced by a new, much more boring-looking building in 1968.

The Bell Inn on the corner of Vicarage Road and Old Church Road, Harborne. A very popular village pub, relatively unchanged to this day despite the growth of Harborne as a dormitory suburb of Birmingham, its position close to the parish church offers some protection from development of its road. It retains its bowling green behind the building, parts of which probably date back to the eighteenth century. The licensee in 1899 was William Butler.

The Duke of York Hotel, Harborne. Situated on the corner of the High Street and Lordswood Road, this closed as recently as 2002 and was demolished to make way for houses on its large, prime site. In 1899 the licensee was Frederick Lewis.

The Golden Cross Hotel, Harborne, 7 May 1924. Located on the corner of Harborne Park Road and Metchley Lane, it was replaced a few years later by a larger, red-brick building more akin to a roadhouse; renamed the Lazy Fox in the 1980s, it became yet another Firkin pub a decade later. Now the Golden Cross once more, it is currently closed and its future uncertain.

The Green Man, Harborne, 14 September 1939. The view is looking up the High Street away from Birmingham with the other end of Metchley Lane on the left and the start of Nursery Road off to the right. Just visible beyond Grays Road corner on the right is the Plough, still much the same today. It was replaced by a new building the very next year.

The (new) Green Man on the same site in 1965. The view is in the opposite direction to the previous photograph with the chapel of the Blue Coat School just visible beyond. This is the latest in a succession of pubs on the site going back to at least 1834. Note the unusual sign on the corner of the building.

The Green Man's sign, 1965. The name is a venerable one for village pubs with early signs depicting the pagan image of a grotesque green head sprouting foliage. This was later often replaced by a portrait of Robin Hood in his Lincoln green; here a green-jacketed hunter has been substituted in a further eradication of its original meaning. The sign is still *in situ*.

The New Inn, Harborne, c. 1960. On the corner of Greenfield Road and Vivian Road and dating from early in the nineteenth century, this is one of Harborne's oldest pubs but, at the time of the photograph, was looking somewhat rundown. In the early 1990s it was taken over from M&B by Banks and its three rooms refurbished sympathetically. Like the Bell, it retains its bowling green and clubhouse.

The Sportsman in Metchley Lane, Harborne, c. 1960. The pub was once famed for its gooseberry growing contests. In keeping with its name, it boasts its own cricket club.

The White Horse in York Street, Harborne, again c. 1960. The building beyond, on the corner of the High Street, is the 1881 Board School (later an Adult Education Centre). The White Horse has been a pub since 1861. The pub now boasts its own in-house brewerry, one of a small but growing number in Birmingham.

Ye Olde House at Home, Lordswood Road, towards the end of the nineteenth century. Running between the villages of Harborne and Bearwood, the road name was then spelt Lord's Wood and was little more than a country lane.

A closer view of the pub about the same time. It was later demolished and replaced by a not unattractive, large, red brick and stone roadhouse serving the area's new residential estates built during the inter-war period. The site is now the corner of Gillhurst Road. The couple outside are probably the licensee and his wife.

The Ivy House Hotel, on the corner of Soho Road and Whitehall Road, Handsworth when it was still very much a village inn set amidst the surrounding trees, cobbles and old cottages, and the taking of a photograph was still very much an event. See also p. 85.

The Woodman Inn, Holyhead Road, Handsworth, 18 January 1900. The side legend reads: GOOD STABLING & BOWLING GREEN. A flag flies from the chimney pot, above the chalked message on the stack: ONE FROM THE FRONT – a reference to the Second Boer War then in progress. Two carters appear to be waiting outside for a drink.

The Billesley Arms, on the corner of Brook Lane and Wheeler's Lane, King's Heath, 1925. The horsecarts are now motor lorries – and their drivers are inside the pub? Another 1*d* weighing machine is located round the side.

The Cross Guns Hotel in King's Heath, an F. Everitt & Co. establishment. It would appear to be high summer and the doors are open invitingly. The cast iron structure on the left is a public urinal, once a common sight on the city streets though only a handful remain *in situ* today.

Inside the Hare & Hounds on King's Heath High Street, March 1975. A timeless scene with its traditional pub furniture and tiled walls. Formerly a Holt's pub, it was rebuilt in 1907 on the site of an earlier pub and, although surviving today, has been subject to a number of interior alterations over the years. Happily, none have been too drastic – so far.

The Horse Shoe Inn on Millpool Hill on Alcester Road South, just beyond the Stratford-on-Avon Canal bridge, on 26 April 1938. Within a few months the cottages on the left had been demolished.

The Green at King's Norton, *c.* 1900. The Bull's Head Inn is on the left, the Saracen's Head Hotel centre and St Nicholas' church right. Today The Green is now shaded by mature trees and encroached on by new buildings.

The Bull's Head, 1896. Staff, customers, passers-by and even neighbours pose for the camera. The licensee was Thomas Chaplin. The pub's name is now carried by a mock-Tudor roadhouse, built immediately adjacent in 1901.

Outside the Navigation Inn, Wharf Road, King's Norton, *c.* 1900. On the left of the trio is Thomas Chaplin of the Bull's Head, in the centre is Hubert Summers, a baker on The Green, and right is Bill (William Thomas) Walker, landlord of the Navigation, which still stands close to the busy Pershore Road South.

Outside the Navigation Inn again, *c.* 1880. The landlady at the time was Mary Rogers, a licensed brewer; her name appears on the lamp and over the door and she is almost certainly one of the women in the doorway. The figures' costumes are indicative of an earlier period than the previous photograph – especially the men's hats.

On the terrace of the Bell Inn, formerly on The Green. The photograph was taken to record the historic occasion of a celebration to mark the ending of the First World War (or the Great War, as it was then labelled). Almost certainly a meal, speeches and endless toasts would have been on the agenda with the villagers – all men – attired in their Sunday best. Such celebrations, either in November 1918 after the Armistice between the Allies and Germany or in 1919, following the signing of the Treaty of Versailles on 29 June that year, were repeated in their thousands in pubs up and down the land.

Outside the Bell Inn again, this time at the front of the building, probably in the 1930s. Members of the Birmingham Walking Club are gathered at what was their training headquarters (by then known as Ye Olde Bell Inn). From left to right the walkers are: -?-, Albert Hobbis, George Nash, Walter Hobbis, landlord James Fletcher, Fred Smith (the club captain), -?-, -?-, Lacey Morris. The other gentlemen are probably committee members and club officials. The window boxes were donated by M&B to the pub – and to the other properties around The Green.

The Plumber's Arms, King's Norton. Another long-vanished pub on The Green, it is decked out with flags and bunting either in celebration of the end of the First World War or, more probably, the Coronation of King George V in 1911.

Customers outside the Plumber's Arms, c. 1912. It is possibly the same occasion as above with benches – and even pot plants – brought out for the group photograph and everyone again in their best clothes. The licensee, Ann R. Kimberley, is probably standing in the doorway.

The Saracen's Head on The Green, in the early twentieth century. The licensee, George Frederick Coombes, is standing centre left with his sons George and Alex.

The Saracen's Head, 18 June 1937. In 1920 the pub's licence was withdrawn and the building given to the church. In 1926 the pub's licence was withdrawn and four years later the building was given to St Nicholas' church (seen behind). Much of the building's half-timbering has been plastered over and all traces of its having once been a hostelry have gone.

Inside the Saracen's Head, 1933. A group of parishioners sit down for a Shrove Tuesday meal, presided over by the vicar – presumably the Revd Canon Thomas Shelton Dunn, vicar of St Nicolas'. Judging by the place settings, the principal fare on offer would appear to be the traditional pancake.

The Saracen's Head in the 1970s, as seen from the churchyard, looking very spick and span. Since its 2000s restoration it has formed part of the St Nicholas' community centre.

The Bull's Head, Moseley, c. 1875. Situated at the heart of Moseley village on St Mary's Row with St Mary's church behind, its sign appears to read R. WALTHEW late of the GLASSMAKERS ARMS, GRANVILLE ST. The road layout around what was the village green is much the same today – only much, more busier – and the buildings have altered somewhat, the Bull's Head for one having been rebuilt in the ornate, red brick style of the Edwardian era when so many of Birmingham's Georgian and Victorian pubs were given a new lease of life. It is as popular today as it ever was (and has regular music nights in an upstairs room), and is one of several thriving pubs in a vibrant district that still retains much of the feel of a village.

The Prince of Wales on the Alcester Road in Moseley, towards the end of the nineteenth century. The licensee was William Haynes. Again rebuilt at an early date, it is a very popular multi-room pub of the traditional kind.

The Old Bell House on the Bristol Road, Northfield. Formerly the Bell Inn, it was demolished in the 1960s. The licensee in 1899 was James Foster.

The Great Stone Inn, Church Road, Northfield, New Year's Eve 1936. Viewed from the gateway of St Laurence's church, the Great Stone of its name is prominent on the corner of the pavement. The pub building, formerly a house, is medieval in origin.

The Great Stone Inn, looking towards the church, probably in the 1960s. Next to the pub is the old village pound where, for safety reasons, the Great Stone is now kept.

Three views of Rednal pubs, beginning with the Barracks Inn, Rednal. At the foot of the Lickey Hills, this has long been a popular spot for Brummies keen to escape into the neighbouring countryside, if only for a day. Here an Edwardian party is at ease, doubtless admiring the view.

The Hare & Hounds on the Lickey Road. An early motor bus stands outside.

The Old Rose & Crown on Rose Hill (now the B4096), Rednal, at the foot of Beacon Hill. Although just over the Birmingham boundary, it has been included here for its close connection with the city, beginning life as it did as a coaching inn where fresh horses could be found to tackle the hills on what was the main Birmingham–Bromsgrove road. As was the eighteenth-century custom, it also served as a courthouse (with the more unfortunate felons being hanged outside). Later, it too was a very pleasant place for Brummies to escape to and is still very much in business.

The Vine, Green Lane, Small Heath, c. 1917. Believed to have been one of the oldest surviving pubs in Birmingham until its demolition in 1927, it was built in about 1630.

The Angel Inn, Sparkbrook, *c.* 1870. On the corner of Stratford Road and Lady Pool Lane (now Ladypool Road), this building dates from at least 1830 and is probably much older in origin. Then on the very edge of Birmingham, by a tollgate, it is now on a busy main road (though sadly no longer a pub). From 1908 it was an Atkinson's pub until that firm's takeover by M&B.

The Dogpool Inn on the corner of Dogpool Lane and the Pershore Road. Dating from at least 1870, it was demolished in the 1930s and a bank built on the site.

A new Dogpool was built on the opposite side of the Pershore Road, on the site of the former Ten Acres Tavern. This is the new pub's cellar, flooded after a particularly heavy storm in 1949. The manager, William Eades, looks on despairingly. The pub is currently named the Hibernian, hosting regular rock nights.

The Three Horseshoes Inn, Lower Stirchley Street, Stirchley. Standing next to the old village forge, it is being engulfed by the encroaching suburbs with their ranks of terraced houses and a new electric tramway (opened 1904) to serve them.

The Fox & Goose Hotel, Ward End, *c.* 1900. Sited on the corner of Stechford Road and Heath Road, it advertises a bowling green, good stabling and home-brewed beer. The licensee in 1899 was Edward George Musto.

The Ring o' Bells in Church Road, Yardley. The licensee in 1899 was Benjamin Spittle. The uncommon pub name echoes the children's rhyme 'Ring-a-ring o'roses, a pocket full of posies', though its supposed connection to the seventeenth-century plague that ravaged England is probably fallacious.

# *Four*

# Suburban Roadhouses

One last category of pub remains to be considered: the roadhouse. Occupying a geographical position between the backstreet boozers and the village inns, and on out beyond them to the next ring of villages outside the city boundary, these were large, imposing pubs situated on suburban main roads and drew their clientele not just from local residential developments but, especially, from passing trade. They were deliberately constructed to be as impressive as money allowed in order to attract custom, offering a range of facilities including a public bar, a lounge and often a restaurant and an off-licence. With the dramatic growth in private motoring after the First World War a large car park became a necessity. These were pubs people went out of their way to visit where they would meet friends and relatives for a drink and a meal, especially at weekends and on Bank Holidays.

The Red Lion, Warwick Road, Acock's Green, 17 March 1958. An old-style, double-fronted pub on the main road. The licensee in 1899 was Thomas Horton.

The King's Head on the Hagley Road, Bearwood, 12 June 1967. This is an even grander, mock-Tudor roadhouse complete with an impressive Ansells clock outside – most useful at this important meeting-place of bus routes where the Hagley Road crosses the end-on junction of Lordswood Road and Bearwood Road (the Outer Circle) but it is now gone. Gutted in the early 1990s and turned into 'The Quantum Experience' – a monstrous cross between a gothic church and an amusement arcade selling alcohol – it is now a restaurant.

The Bradford Arms, Castle Bromwich, pre-First World War, when Castle Bromwich was no more than a tiny village on a major route into Birmingham from the northeast and the Bradford Arms was an important watering-hole for farmers, drovers, carters and the like making the journey to and from market. It was demolished in the early 1980s and a new pub built, keeping the old name.

The Earl Grey on the corner of Pershore Road and Balsall Heath Road, 1896. The cab shelter has long gone and the Pershore Road in the foreground is now usually solid with traffic but the pub appears much the same today – except for the fact that it closed in 1998 and its future is uncertain. This whole area, where Edgbaston meets Balsall Heath, is now packed with post-Second World War housing.

The Tyburn House on Kingsbury Road, Erdington. It was superseded by a much larger roadhouse of the same name built by Ansells at the remodelled Chester Road/Kingsbury Road junction in 1930. The licensee at the time of the photograph was Ernest Woodgate.

Ye Olde Green Man in Bromford Lane, Erdington, 18 February 1939. A fairly safe rule to follow is this: be very, very wary of any establishment calling itself 'Ye Olde' something or other. It probably held true seventy years ago as well.

The Cross Keys pub, built 1911, on the corner of Station Road and Erdington High Street, probably in the 1960s. A typical M&B roadhouse with mock-Tudor trimmings, it looks much the same some thirty years on.

The Bull's Head, Stratford Road, Hall Green, 1920s or 1930s. Another M&B establishment.

The Ivy House Hotel on the corner of Soho Road and Ivy Road, Handsworth, 1907. Butlers of Wolverhampton held the licence. This reform pub replaced the former village inn of the same name, depicted on. p.63.

The Red Lion, Handsworth, also on the Soho Road. The original building dated from at least 1829 but was rebuilt by Holt Brewery Co. during the 1900s as a highly-decorated, terracotta-faced hostelry. The interior was no less ornate.

The Villa Cross Inn, Handsworth. Another Holt's pub, this stood at the junction of Villa Road, Heathfield Road and Lozells Road. The licensee was John Ogden.

The Villa Cross again, this time at a slightly earlier date c. 1890. The large painted legend on the front of the building announces that it sells Fox & Co.'s Entire Ales whilst that on the side wall reads: FAMILIES SUPPLIED WITH THE FINEST WINES & SPIRITS BURTON ALE & STOUT IN CASK AND BOTTLE AT WHOLESALE PRICES – quite a comprehensive list in all! According to the lamp over the front door, the licensee was one T. Hale. Note that although the pavements are paved, kerbed and lit by gas lamps, the roads are still unsurfaced – though two tram tracks can just be made out amidst the cart ruts. These were used by horse trams, this route not being electrified until 1906 (and some paving at least put down on the road).

The New Inns Hotel, Handsworth, October 1901. Standing on the corner of Sandwell Road and the Holyhead Road, a new extension has obviously been added (around 1900) to a much older building (which possible dated back to the eighteenth century).

The rear of the New Inns, also in October 1901. Stabling for tramway horses was once provided here, and there was a bowling green – now a car park. The older part of the building was rebuilt the following year in a grand manner. The licence was held by M&B.

The Red Lion in Vicarage Road, King's Heath, c. 1935. Opened in August 1904 it was the first of a very new breed of public house: large, standing alone and of an architectural style very different to that of its immediate predecessors. Faced with Wildon stone at the front, its architect was C.E. Bateman who designed it for the Priory Estate Co. (who leased it to M&B). It deliberately harks back to the ecclesiastical buildings of the late Middle Ages – hardly surprisingly, considering the property company's name – and was a calculated attempt to move the neighbourhood's consumption of alcohol into a new, more acceptable region of respectability away from the village inn or backstreet boozer. It has long been a very popular live music venue.

The Man in the Moon in King's Norton, 1950. A good example of the large but austere roadhouse look. The Man in the Moon is a traditional pub name with a sign depicting either a face on the moon or a man sitting in its crescent; since the 1969 moon landing some signs at pubs with this name have been repainted to depict an astronaut on the lunar surface.

The Saddlers Arms, Aldridge Road, Perry Barr, April 1959. Formerly standing near the corner of Franchise Street, it was demolished shortly afterwards to make way for the Birchfield Road underpass – a not unusual case of the road it was built to serve being responsible for a pub's destruction.

The Crown & Cushion at the junction of Birchfield Road with Wellington Road and Aston Lane (the Outer Circle), again April 1959. Named from the much smaller Old Crown & Cushion on the opposite side of Birchfield Road, this roadhouse survived the building of the underpass (though the widened road now runs extremely close to the frontage of the pub).

The Black Horse on the Bristol Road South in Northfield, in the 1960s. Built by Davenports in 1929, this was the epitome of a mock-Tudor Midlands mansion house re-worked as a public house – complete with bowling green and separate refreshment room – with its stepped roofline, jutting bays and gables, towering brick chimney stacks and silver-grey timbering (later repainted jet black as the false image of Elizabethan building has it). It is undoubtedly one of the grandest buildings of its kind in the whole of England, even eighty years on, though its present-day setting on a major road detracts somewhat from its majesty. The architect was Francis Goldsbrough of the firm of Bateman and Bateman, who were noted for their work on a number of other local pubs. Since 2010 it has been part of the popular Wetherspoon chain.

The Holly Bush on the Hagley Road, Quinton, 14 September 1926. A new carriageway has just been built to the right of the old road; this was later replaced by a dual carriageway and the pub demolished, replaced in 1937 by a larger building of the same name by the junction with Quinton Road. After several changes of name, it now trades as the Quinton Toby Carvery.

Looking down the Bristol Road towards Selly Oak, 1925. The Gun Barrels pub is in the middle distance on the right, just past the junction with Edgbaston Park Road. Always popular with students from the adjacent university, the pub survived the widening of the Bristol Road into a dual carriageway – though half a century later it was rebuilt and its bowling green destroyed. It was demolished in 2013 to make way for the new University of Birmingham Sports Centre.

Another Bristol Road pub in Selly Oak, this time the Oak Inn. One of Selly Oak's oldest pubs, it closed in 1983, another victim of road widening. (Its nearby replacement, the Great Oak, only lasted from 1985 to 1994!)

The Mermaid Inn, Sparkhill, c. 1880. It stood on the corner where the Stratford Road (right) met the Warwick Road (left), a major junction then as now, where two important Birmingham arterial roads meet. The building was an eighteenth-century conversion of a seventeenth-century one, becoming a pub in 1751 or even earlier.

The Mermaid, *c.* 1910. The old pub had been demolished and a new one erected on the site in 1895 while the whole surrounding area was developed with rows of prosperous Victorian/Edwardian villas and shops. It was rebuilt again in 1949 after suffering damage during the Second World War.

The Breedon Cross Hotel, Stirchley. This distinctively-shaped pub stood on the Pershore Road, just beyond the Worcester & Birmingham Canal bridge. Derelict for several years after it closed (as the Breedon Bar), it was demolished in the early 2000s to make way for housing.

The Bull's Head Hotel, Yardley. Sited on the Coventry Road in the Hay Mills area of Yardley, the pub is not so far removed both stylistically and geographically from the 1895 Mermaid (p. 99). The licensee in 1897 was one Rabbi Russell. It closed in 1983, yet another victim of road widening.

# Five

# *The Woodman –*
# *a Warning*

*This Section is devoted to just one pub, the Woodman, which once stood in Easy Row at the very heart of political power in Birmingham, close to both the Town Hall and the Council House. Indeed, before the latter building was completed in 1879 the pub served as the unofficial meeting place for the Council – and even, during the 1850s, as the official one. In 1891–2 the old Woodman was rebuilt by Henry Naden as a truly splendid example of a late-Victorian period city pub with magnificent tiled decoration both inside and out, a proud embodiment of Birmingham's newly-granted city status. Less than fourscore years later it had gone, like so much of Birmingham's reputation. Coincidence? I think not. And the warning? Simply this: if an historical and architectural gem such as the Woodman can be swept away, what price any others save eternal vigilance?*

Easy Row, shortly after the Second World War. This official photograph was taken in readiness for the redevelopment of the area when the street was obliterated to make way for Paradise Circus. The Woodman is sandwiched between a booksellers and a furniture store.

The pub's front façade, 6 June 1952. The use of a statue (carved in stone by A.E. Naylor) in place of a more conventional hanging board was a deliberate harking-back to an earlier age when inns and taverns often made use of three-dimensional signs.

The Easy Row entrance to the Woodman, 1964. The door to the Public Bar is on the left, that to the Private Bar in the centre and the entrance to the Smoke Room on the right. The sumptuous decoration of the façade can be clearly seen while the display of bottles and advertising placards in the windows adds a genteel touch.

Inside the Public Bar, 13 July 1964. The bar itself is refreshingly uncluttered when compared with its modern counterparts, and the floor is bare in accordance with the usual practice. Sawdust would be scattered and then swept up to remove cigarette ends, matches, spilt beer and the like.

The tiled panel on the left wall of the entrance, 13 July 1964, with the eponymous woodman depicted as hard at work. The following photographs were all taken on the same day.

The tiled panel on the right hand wall of the entrance, with the woodman now resting from his labours, waistcoat off, forever waiting for the pub to open. He is portrayed as being considerably younger than his statue counterpart, probably a result of lack of communication between the factories responsible for the panels' production and the architect. The notice over the Smoke Room door proclaims the licensee to be Victor Richard Timms.

Inside the Private Bar. The floor is still bare but the customers are now provided with upholstered stools. The swivelling, head-height 'snob-screens' over the bar counter were there to shield customers discussing business, or enjoying a furtive liaison, from prying eyes. Extremely rare to find nowadays, they were only opened when drinks were being ordered. The single beer pump on the counter indicates that the landlord expected to serve drinks other than an endless succession of pints. The painted windows continue the pub's bucolic theme.

The wonderful wood and stained glass screens in the passageway behind the Smoke Room door. Smoke Rooms were traditionally cordoned-off from the Public Bar and were the province of (accompanied) ladies and white collar workers such as clerks and shopworkers anxious to preserve their superiority in status over the lowly labourers and unskilled artisans in the Public.

The Smoke Room with its much smaller counter – patrons would be expected to sit and drink, rather than linger at the bar as in the Public. (Some pubs would even offer a waiter service at your table.) There is no hand pump on the bar – any pints requested would have to be pulled in one of the other rooms.

Looking down the length of the Smoke Room. The full extent of the interior decoration can now be appreciated while the difference in status between here and the Public is emphasized further by the more comfortable seating and the tile-patterned floor.

The grand side fireplace in the Smoke Room with its arrangement of tables, benches and chairs creating a semi-private enclave for a small group to relax in.

The equally impressive end fireplace, designed to serve a similar purpose.

What it may have lacked in comfort, the Woodman's Public Bar famously made up for in decor, notably its set of tiled pictures of old Birmingham scenes, six of which can be seen here on the wall. Not only the rest of the wall space but even the ceiling was tiled!

Looking back the other way down the Public towards the Easy Row entrance door.

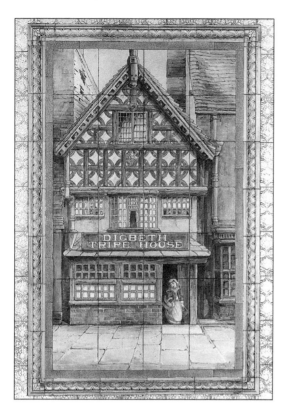

The next ten photographs show the tiled pictures on the wall of the Public in close-up, beginning with the old Tripe House eating-house in Well Street, Digbeth.

Prince Rupert's entry into Deritend, 1642, with the Golden Lion pub in the background (see pp 16-17).

The Old Crown public house with Cavaliers parading in the street (see p. 10).

The Ship Inn at Camp Hill, Prince Rupert's headquarters (see p. 13).

The Hen & Chickens public house in New Street (see p. 26).

Looking up Hill Street to Birmingham Town Hall (its elevation decidedly exaggerated). Opened in 1834, this attractive building was reopened in 2007 after a lengthy, multi-million pound refurbishment; from the same vantage point today – roughly the northern end of New Street station – it is sadly obscured by modern office blocks.

St Martin's Lane in Digbeth, just south of the Bull Ring, in 1840, with the boundary wall to St Martin's church on the right and the Swan with Two Nicks on the left. (For the origins of this curious pub name, see p. 45.) Apart from the church, all the buildings seen here have long been swept away.

A very familiar Birmingham scene: the view across the old Bull Ring market place towards St Martin's Church. Today the buildings are brand new but the vista remains.

An external view of Aston Hall during Cavalier occupancy . . .

. . . and an internal view showing minor Civil War damage – or just the aftermath of a rather good party? (The building suffered a three-day siege in 1643 when in the hands of the Royalists.) A grand Elizabethan manor house, set in its own park, Aston Hall is now the property of the city and a popular visitor attraction.

# Six

# Last Orders

In 1964-5 Birmingham Council's Public Works Department undertook a photographic survey of the public houses in the area bounded by Broad Street and Lee Bank to the north-west and south-west, and Suffolk Street and Bristol Street to the east, prior to much of the area being cleared to make way for road widening and new housing. Photographs of no less than twenty-seven of the now-demolished pubs exist and are reproduced here, in alphabetical order of their names, together with details of their locations, as a roll call of the fallen. (Photographs of the handful that survived the clearances can be found in Section Two.)

The Anchor Inn on the corner of Islington Row and Tennant Street, 1965. A typical, no-nonsense backstreet boozer which, like so many of its kind, has been bulldozed away – in this case, to make way for the Five Ways Shopping Centre.

The Bell on the corner of Bell Barn Road and Bristol Street, 1965. It is still sporting its Butlers Ales sign though, as with many of these premises pictured here, the pub sign has gone.

The Bell Barn Tavern on the corner of Bell Barn Road and Ryland Road, 1964. According to the mandatory notice over the door, the licensee at this date was William George Foster.

The Black Lion on Smallbrook Street, 1965. The street no longer exists though the name lives on in Smallbrook Queensway.

The Bowling Green, Holloway Head, 1964. A seemingly unusual name for a pub – but, as mentioned earlier, a green was at one time an important feature of many Birmingham and Black Country hostelries.

The Britannia on the corner of Latimer Street and Piggot Street, 1965. Both streets were about to be wiped from the map. Smith's beer was formerly brewed by Frederick Smith Ltd at the Aston Model Brewery (established 1875) based at 251 Lichfield Road, Aston. The licensee is given as Cyril Thomas Allen.

The Colmore Arms in Latimer Street, 1964. Note the separate outdoor entrance for off-licence sales: an important part of a backstreet licensee's trade came from serving those who wanted a 'take-out' or 'carry-out' to drink at home. The pub name commemorates the Colmore family, owners of the local New Hall Estate (and in connection with whom Colmore Row and New Hall Street are named).

The Edgbaston on the corner of Lee Bank Road and Ryland Road, 1964. The former road was greatly widened to become Lee Bank Middleway. The licensee was John Francis Goodman.

The Edgbaston Tavern in Lee Bank Road, 1964. Like the Edgbaston, the Edgbaston Tavern took its name from the Birmingham district immediately to the south-west. The signboard, if there ever was one, has gone but the name remains etched on the windows. The licensee was Harry Cale.

The Glassmakers' Arms on the corner of Granville Street and Holliday Street, 1964. It took its name from one of the principal trades of this particular area of the city.

The Gough Arms on the corner of Sun Street West and Spring Street (not to be confused with the nearby Gough Arms depicted in Section Two, p. 51), 1964. A remnant of Spring Street survives, Sun Street West does not. The licensee was Clifford Raymond Watts.

The Grand Junction where Great Colmore Street met Bell Barn Road, 1964. The licensee was Albert Stokes and the area is now a housing development.

The King's Arms on the corner of Bishopgate Street and William Street, 1964. The licensee was Harry Edward Eccles. The roadways are still there but the pub is not.

The Nottingham Arms on the corner of Bristol Street and Bristol Passage, 1964. The entire length of this west side of Bristol Street was demolished to make way for the present second carriageway. The licensee was George James Middleton.

The Queen's Stores, built 1908, on the corner of Bath Row and Piggot Street, 1964.

The Red Cow in Bristol Street, 1964.

The Roebuck on the corner of St Martin's Street and William Street, 1965.

The Shakespearian Bar on the corner of Great Colmore Street and Cregoe Street, 1965.

The Sun Inn on the corner of Sun Street and Bristol Street, 1964. Sun Street was another casualty of the widening of Bristol Street. The licensee was Ronald Francis Greatrix.

The Swan Inn on the corner of Bell Barn Road and Wynn Street, 1964. The traditional lamp on the corner of the pub has vanished, but its ornate bracket survives.

The Trees Hotel on the corner of Bath Row and Wheeley's Lane, 1965. The decorative frieze under the eaves is in marked contrast to the austere art deco look of the ground floor exterior.

The Unicorn on the corner of Holloway Head and Speaking Stile Walk, 1964. The licensee is given as Alfred Henry Thomas.

The Victoria Inn in Bristol Street, 1964. The licensee was Alfred Ernest Clark.

The Welcome Inn on the corner of Owen Street and Wheeley's Lane, 1964. Owen Street has since been redeveloped out of existence. A good example of the tiny corner pub, little larger than the next door houses. Licensee was George Edwin Pryor.

The Wheatsheaf on the corner of Irving Street and Latimer Street, 1964. The licensee was Derek Newton Tilley.

The White Horse in William Street, 1964. The low brick structure in the side yard is almost certainly the outside gent's toilet – yet another traditional pub feature well down the road to extinction.

The Woodman on the corner of Irving Street and Cregoe Street, 1965. The site is unrecognizable today following the foreshortening of Irving Street.

New counters for old: the National Provincial Bank on the corner of Bennett's Hill and Waterloo Street, 1974. This final, apparently unrelated photograph has been included because, in marked contrast to the rest of this section, it offers a bright ray of hope for the future. The last half of the 1990s has seen a rash of new pubs opened in the business district of the city centre, conversions of former financial premises. Several have been done sympathetically in keeping with the existing architecture and internal decor of the buildings in order to reproduce the type of grand, spacious bar that once graced our city centre – in this case, Bennetts. 'Last Orders' have definitely not yet been called for the pubs of Birmingham.

# Worth a Visit

*Just how successfully the 1990s' generation of new city pubs – principally conversions of redundant bank and building society premises – will integrate themselves into Birmingham's social scene is as yet uncertain. Despite a plague of unsuitable refurbishments of the last three decades, a handful of pubs do – miraculously – survive in the city centre relatively unchanged from their original state, and still serving real, cask-conditioned ales. Even so, from large to small, from grand to functional, they manage to cover a wide range of size, architecture and decor. This is not a long list and, sadly, likely to become even shorter with each passing year as one area after another is redeveloped.*

Definitely worth a visit, within the concrete confines of the Inner Ring Road, are:

The **Old Contemptibles**: corner of Edmund Street and Livery Street.
The **Old Royal**: corner of Church Street and Cornwall Street.
The **Victoria**: corner of John Bright Street and Station Street.
The **Wellington**: Bennett's Hill (for the best selection of real ales in Birmingham).

A few other authentic frontages can still be found in the city centre – but beware: they can hide a multitude of horrors!

Immediately beyond the Inner Ring Road the situation improves immeasurably with many unspoilt backstreet pubs tucked away in the old manufacturing districts. Birmingham's industries, at least in the nineteenth century, tended to be compartmentalized into specific areas of the old town, which then became known by the name of that particular trade; perhaps the most famous is the Jewellery Quarter with the most recent addition the Chinese Quarter. Within easy walking distance of the city centre, the following are recommended to all those seeking to experience something of the true flavour of Birmingham's traditional public houses while it can still be found and savoured. Grouped by location, they are:

## Chinese Quarter

The **Old Fox**: Hurst Street.

## Digbeth

The **Anchor**: corner of Bradford Street and Rea Street.
The **Lamp Tavern**: Barford Street.
The **Woodman**: corner of Albert Street and New Canal Street.

## Gun Quarter

The **Bull**: corner of Price Street and Loveday Street.

## Jewellery Quarter

The **Church Inn**: corner of Great Hampton Street and Harford Street.

## Ladywood

The **Craven Arms**: corner of Gough Street and Blucher Street.
The **City Tavern**: corner of Bishopgate Street and Tennant Street.

## St Pauls

The **Queen's Arms**: corner of Newhall Street and Charlotte Street.
The **Shakespeare**: corner of Summer Row and Lionel Street.